James Baldwin

PETER PANIC

OBERON BOOKS
LONDON

WWW.OBERONBOOKS.COM

First published in 2012 by Oberon Books Ltd
521 Caledonian Road, London N7 9RH
Tel: +44 (0) 20 7607 3637 / Fax: +44 (0) 20 7607 3629
e-mail: info@oberonbooks.com
www.oberonbooks.com

A catalogue record for this book is available from the British Library.

PB ISBN: 978-1-84943-471-3
Digital ISBN: 978-1-84943-640-3

Cover image by Tom Guy (www.tomguy.co.uk)

Visit www.oberonbooks.com to read more about all our books
and to buy them. You will also find features, author interviews and
news of any author events, and you can sign up for e-newsletters
so that you're always first to hear about our new releases.

James Baldwin would like to thank all the people who have made this project possible:

Michael and Pauline Baldwin for their love and support, Elgiva Field and Rachel Bagshaw for putting up with me, Leah Larkin and The London Eye for supporting function theatre's commitment to accessibility, Purni Morell for her continued expertise, Elizabeth Newman for listening, Oberon Books for printing my words, Giles Smart for expert guidance and James Guy for being a wonderful, wonderful man.

Characters

STEPHEN
early 30s

WENDY
early 30s

PETER
an adolescent

The place is London. The time is tomorrow.

During the audience incoming a SFX plays on loop. A distorted emergency broadcast news bulletin:

> **This is an all channel World-cast message:**
> **Stay in your homes, lock all doors and windows.**
> **Curfew is active. Do not leave your homes.**
> **A woman has been found, her unborn child**
> **ripped from her womb, things can't get any worse.**
> **You must stay at home. Curfew is active.**

A child's bedroom on the upper floor of a large Victorian town house. The room is messy and untidy with children's games and half completed arts and crafts projects. Clothes drawers are pulled open and their contents are strewn all around. There is an empty laundry basket yet there are plenty of dirty clothes. Up stage is a large open window besides which is an air conditioning unit. Through the window we can see it is dusk – this is the only source of light. We can hear a large angry crowd in the streets nearby. Throughout the play the sound of unrest grows, gunshots, sirens and helicopters are heard intermittently. The Westminster Chimes introduce the passing of the hour and we hear Big Ben toll eleven times.

A man, STEPHEN, enters. He flicks the light switch by the door, nothing happens. He steps through the detritus and stands by the open window looking out. He unfastens a few buttons of his shirt and untucks it from his trousers. He tries to encourage air flow by moving the fabric. He kicks the air conditioning unit. A woman enters, WENDY, she wears a sympathetic smile.

WENDY: Is she dead?

STEPHEN: Not yet.

WENDY: Have they found it?

STEPHEN: No.

            Where's Peter?

WENDY: Playing.

STEPHEN: It's eleven gone.

WENDY: He's playing.

STEPHEN: The little shit.

WENDY: It's still light.

15

STEPHEN: I wish this thing would work.

WENDY: No power.

STEPHEN: So hot.

WENDY: Still.

STEPHEN: Still?

WENDY: The weather will break soon.

STEPHEN: Why's it here anyway? By the window?
          Who put it here?

WENDY: The man.

STEPHEN: What man?

WENDY: The staff.

STEPHEN: Who? There aren't many left.

WENDY: Does it matter?

STEPHEN: Yes, why did he put it by the window?

WENDY: The drainage pipe goes out.

STEPHEN: Through the window?
          Retard.

WENDY: Stephen!

STEPHEN: No wonder there's no power,
          we're trying to cool the fucking country.

WENDY: I thought you didn't use that word.

STEPHEN: Well,
          we're no longer a nation Wendy.

WENDY: No.

STEPHEN: What a fucking mess.

WENDY: You'll think of something.

STEPHEN: In here. What a fucking mess in here.

WENDY: I'll ask him to tidy.

STEPHEN: Ask him? Tell him.

WENDY: I will.

STEPHEN: He's a pig.

WENDY: He's thirteen.

STEPHEN: Bastard.

WENDY: Stephen. Don't talk about your child like that.

STEPHEN: He's not my child.

WENDY: My child like that.

STEPHEN: He's not.

WENDY: My baby.

STEPHEN: We've only had him a year.

WENDY: I love him.

STEPHEN: He's feral.

WENDY: My baby.

STEPHEN: It's eleven at night, the city's in riot,
the country's collapsing, curfew, where's Peter?
Wild with the dogs.

WENDY: London's not Athens.

STEPHEN: Yet.

Wendy, after tonight we'll be just as fucked.

WENDY: I wish you wouldn't swear.

STEPHEN: Cunt.

WENDY: Stephen!

STEPHEN: This is mine, he's taken it.

STEPHEN holds up a pornographic magazine.

WENDY: I'm your wife!

STEPHEN: Don't be so proper.

WENDY: It's wholly improper.

STEPHEN: That he's thieved it, I know.

WENDY: That you have it.

STEPHEN: But I don't have it because he took it.

WENDY: There shouldn't be hardcore porn in the house.

STEPHEN: It was hidden. It's not even that hard.
             Look.

WENDY: I don't want to look.

STEPHEN: But he took it!

WENDY: I think you're missing the point.

STEPHEN: The point is
             he's a thief, a liar, and not to be trusted.

WENDY: He's thirteen.

STEPHEN: Is he? But how do we know?
             He's like a dog from the kennel we've guessed
             his age.

WENDY: He is thirteen Stephen, I know.

STEPHEN: So he's thirteen is he Wendy? Good job;
             that's been the answer ever since we got him.
             He's dirty, he's thirteen, he's a thief, he's
             thirteen, he microwaved our cat, he's thirteen,
             you hide all the kitchen knives, thirteen,
             he pissed on our bed; my side not yours, why?
             Because he's thirteen.

WENDY: He is just a boy.

STEPHEN: No Wendy, he's thirteen.

             (.)

WENDY: This life is very different than the one
             he had before.

STEPHEN: Wendy, how do you know?
             He says he can't remember.

WENDY: He forgets.
             Peter forgets, he just needs reminding.

STEPHEN: Reminding of what? That he no longer
             lives wild? That he no longer toilets outdoors?
             That he's not a dog? He needs to remind me.
             Last night I had a dream, shall I tell you?

We were on holiday, remember those?
We were sat by the swim pool me and you.
There were some kids playing over to the right.
They were sat at this water picnic bench thing;
it had built-in taps, fountains, water guns,
they were playing at water fights, splashing.
Some dogs came, the kids started squirting them,
they were all wagging tails at first, biting
at the water, they were glad to be cooled.
But then one of the kids took it too far,
it stopped being this watery bench thing
and became a military water cannon,
this kid was bashing the dogs with the hose.
The dogs started snapping, yelping, running,
they crossed to the other side of the pool,
directly opposite where we were sat.
There was a kid in the water crying,
trying to get out, scared, and this one dog
ran past, and as it did, it whipped around
clamping the child's head in its jaws, dragging
this babe from the pool. I could see the flesh
tearing, cheek being ripped from jowl, you were
crying but I could hear this laugh laughing,
someone was loving it, enjoying it,
a lot. My eyes searched the panicked pool side
and do you know who I saw? Sitting there?
I saw Peter, sat, mongrels surrounding,
Peter, he was laughing, laughing, laughing
as dogs did his bidding, laughing Wendy.
Peter was laughing.

WENDY: Was he laughing Stephen?

STEPHEN: You can take the piss all you want Wendy
but dreams that vivid are rarely for nought.

WENDY: You were just processing everything that
happened yesterday.

STEPHEN: It is more than that.
Why does Peter play, run wild with the dogs?

WENDY: Because he's thirteen.

STEPHEN: There you go again.

WENDY: Because he's thirteen and the children that
weren't adopted have been removed, evacuated,
by your government, and the children that
were adopted have left the city with
their new parents. He's on his own. The dogs
are his friends.

STEPHEN: Perhaps we should let him go
and play permanently, who are we to
deny him friendship?

WENDY: His parents. He'll learn.

STEPHEN: He stole my magazine.

WENDY: Which you shouldn't have.

STEPHEN: Why?

WENDY: Because it sets a bad example.

STEPHEN: It's relaxing! Nobody's bothered if
the Prime Minister masturbates. Have you
heard what they're chanting? It seems they're fully
aware I'm a wanker. We're all at it.
Baby battering pictures of Stacey
from Essex, makes no odds when you're on the
verge of a coup.

WENDY: You're so vile.

STEPHEN: Just middle class.

*STEPHEN's phone beeps multiple times as messages arrive in
quick succession.*

He reads his text messages, putting the magazine down.

STEPHEN: The network's being rebooted, it worked.
The power is about to be restored.
There's an increase in assassination

chatter. Foxtrot has been convened. She died. I should go.

WENDY: Stephen please get rid of that.

STEPHEN: Don't stress, in fact you can have it. Relax.

He kisses her and exits.

WENDY is alone on stage. She looks across to the magazine then begins to tidy the bedroom; folding the clean clothes back into drawers. We hear a burst of gun fire in the distance. She tidies some of the toys into a toy chest. She pauses to fan herself with a cardboard 'snakes and ladders' board. She collects dirty laundry into the basket, sniffing some clothes to check their cleanliness. She smells a pair of boxer shorts. She sniffs at them again. She stops herself. She tries to distract herself by picking up the pornographic magazine. She sits on the bed. She idly looks at the magazine. She puts the magazine down and reaches for the underwear again. She inhales through the underwear. She runs her hand up her inner thigh beneath her dress. She places the underwear underneath her dress, using it to masturbate. As she masturbates the power is restored, we know this because in every electric wall socket there is a night light plug which suddenly illuminates. At the same time a boy, PETER, appears at the bedroom window unnoticed. He has a backpack. He watches WENDY climax, as she does he howls like a wolf which startles WENDY.

PETER: *(Howls.)*

WENDY: Peter.

PETER: Wendy, you shouldn't be in here.

WENDY: How long have you been there?

PETER: Long enough to know I have a new pair of lucky pants.

WENDY: I was just...

PETER: I know what you were doing. They wet?

WENDY: I'm your mother.

21

PETER: I excite you.

WENDY: Peter stop.

PETER: You're the one that broke the rule.
          Your own rule Wendy.

WENDY: I've done no such thing.

PETER: I just caught you.

WENDY: Yes but we haven't…

PETER: Touched?
          You can't hide your thimbles from me forever.
          I know you want to.

WENDY: No Peter.

PETER: Just one
          little thimble.

WENDY: Peter no.

PETER: On the lips.

He is about to kiss her. WENDY moves away.

WENDY: It's too hot in here.

PETER: I like it. I smell
          you, and him.

WENDY: He's your father.

PETER: Daddy?

WENDY: Yes.

PETER: That's impossible.

WENDY: Why?

PETER: 'cause I'm Daddy
          and you're Mummy. That man isn't playing,
          it's my game.

WENDY: Stephen.

PETER: I forget his name.

WENDY: This game's different Peter. I'm your mother.

PETER: I'm not a baby.

WENDY: You're my little boy.

PETER: It's boring. Let's play the more grown up game.

WENDY: I thought you didn't like the grown up things.

PETER: Come on, you're Mummy and you say things like
'hard day at work dear?, kettle's on the blink,
there was another power cut today,
can I have a cheque book of my own please?'
And as Daddy I reply 'inflation
at forty-eight per cent, twenty-four million
unemployed, the hospital's burning down,
suck my…'.

WENDY: Peter!

PETER: You started it Wendy.

WENDY: I shouldn't be in here.

WENDY starts to leave.

PETER: Don't forget your porn.

(.)

*PETER offers the porn. WENDY takes it. She opens the top
drawer of the chest of drawers. She places the magazine inside
and then slowly closes it.*

(.)

WENDY turns to leave.

PETER: There were pirates in the park.

WENDY: Anarchists.

PETER: One had a hook for a hand.

WENDY: Extremists.

PETER: He reminded me of someone.

WENDY: No, no.

PETER: He had an awfully large crew.

WENDY: Looters.

PETER: They have made their camp all across the park.
From the Palace to Kensington Gardens.
There's not a single patch of green Wendy,
the trees don't seem to mind; they were laughing
and joking with the pirates.

WENDY: There's no such
thing as pirates.

PETER: We both know that's not true.

WENDY: They're just poor and hungry.

PETER: Poor, starved and crazed.

WENDY: Daddy will think of something I am sure.

PETER: But Stevie's running out of time.

WENDY: Stephen.

PETER: I heard them say. The one with a hook said
it was time to teach Stevie a lesson.
Tonight. Tonight they're going to get him.

Gun fire is heard in the distance.

PETER: Plastic rounds Mummy?

(.)

WENDY resumes her tidying.

PETER: What you doing?

WENDY: Tidy room, tidy mind.

PETER: It's giving me a headache.

WENDY: Just clearing
away the clutter.

PETER: They're my adventures.

WENDY: And as your mother it's my job.

PETER: Is it?

*As WENDY tidies one item, PETER simultaneously untidies
another. It's playful at first but WENDY becomes increasingly
frustrated whilst PETER enjoys it more and more. At first the*

tidying/untidying takes place at opposite sides of the room, crossing over each other, but as the game progresses they spiral closer until WENDY is trying to take something out of PETER's hand to prevent him adding to the mess.

PETER: Those are my new lucky pants.

WENDY: Please Peter.

PETER: Clammy. I thought I never wanted to be a man but now I'm realising there are other ways to have fun.

WENDY: Peter, I'm a grown woman.

PETER: Wendy, we're the same age.

WENDY: Once maybe.

PETER: In here.

PETER gently places his hand over her heart, touching her breast.

PETER: Tootles almost killed you, but my acorn kiss stopped the arrow.

WENDY: You remember?

PETER: Some things I don't forget.

(.)

WENDY breaks away and continues tidying.

PETER: Wendy, who is Tinkerbell?

WENDY: I don't know.

PETER: I keep having funny dreams about her.

WENDY: You're just saying that.

PETER: Why would I do that?

WENDY: To hurt me.

PETER: So you do know who she is?

WENDY: I have told you. You can't make me jealous.

25

PETER: In my dream she wears even fewer leaves
than she used too.

WENDY: It's just your age that's all.

PETER: I wake up feeling funny.

WENDY: Peter.

PETER: Hard.

WENDY: I don't want to know. Stop saying these things.

PETER: You can't hide your thimbles from me forever.

WENDY: Stop. Please. It's my birthday tomorrow.

PETER: Is it?

WENDY: Peter, you know it is.

PETER: Do I?

WENDY: You said you would never forget.

PETER: Did I?

WENDY: Yes!

PETER: You said I wouldn't find you alone
in my room again but I have and you
were. Did you forget?

WENDY: I was with Stephen.

PETER: Stevie?

WENDY: Father.

PETER: We both know I'm Daddy.

(.)

PETER: It's just one little thimble Wendy. Please.

*PETER approaches her. He is just about to kiss her as STEPHEN
enters switching on the light, he is preoccupied so doesn't see
what he's interrupting.*

STEPHEN: Wendy it's time, we have…where have you been?

PETER: Out.

STEPHEN: Out? Out? Adults go 'out'. You're thirteen.

PETER: It's Wendy's birthday tomorrow or have you forgotten?

STEPHEN: Of course I've not forgot.

PETER: Liar.

WENDY: Don't speak to your father like that.

PETER: Stevie's not my father.

WENDY: Peter.

STEPHEN: You stink.
Go and wash.

PETER: You're not my father.

WENDY: Peter!
Please have a bath whilst we have power.

PETER takes off his backpack and drops it amongst the other untidied detritus. He goes to exit.

STEPHEN: Runt.

PETER: *(Growls [as he exits]).*

(.)

STEPHEN: They're attacking paediatricians.

WENDY: Why?

STEPHEN: The same reason they're called baby doctors.

WENDY: But they don't know it was a paedophile.

STEPHEN: He was a nonce.

WENDY: You don't know it's a man.

STEPHEN: Wendy, a woman couldn't have done that.

WENDY: You don't / know.

STEPHEN: To / another woman? With child?

WENDY: Depends how much she wanted a baby.
Have they found it?

STEPHEN: No.

WENDY: Do they think it's dead?

STEPHEN: She was due in September. They are
born earlier than eight months and survive.

WENDY: Born?

STEPHEN: Try not to think about it.

WENDY: I can't not.

STEPHEN: I know.

               (.)

               We hear the Westminster chimes strike the passing of the
               quarter hour.

               The electricity flickers for a moment.

STEPHEN: Wendy, we have to leave. It was the straw
that broke the camel's back.

WENDY: When?

STEPHEN: Tonight.

WENDY: Where?

STEPHEN: The Scandinavian Alliance has
agreed to take us.

WENDY: I'll pack Peter's bag.

STEPHEN: No Wendy, they've agreed harbour for us.
Not Peter.

WENDY: He's my son.

STEPHEN: They know he's not.
They've got too many children as it is,
worse than here.

WENDY: He can work, he's thirteen.

STEPHEN: They've said no.

WENDY: Did you ask?

STEPHEN: Of course I did.

WENDY: So we just leave him? I'll stay.

STEPHEN: You can't.

WENDY: Why?

STEPHEN: Because I've given an order that at
                  midnight tonight you will be by my side,
                  on board a military transport, without
                  Peter.

WENDY: I won't go.

STEPHEN: They'll sedate you.

WENDY: No,
                  we can't.

STEPHEN: There's no other way.

WENDY: You hate him.

STEPHEN: It's not about that.

WENDY: You've not denied it.

STEPHEN: We have to leave the country before we're both
                  disposed of.

WENDY: Stop saying that.

STEPHEN: What?

WENDY: Country.
                  You hate that word.

STEPHEN: The cunt-try hates me. Us.

WENDY: They don't hate Peter.

STEPHEN: He's been kept away
                  from the media, true.

WENDY: You're leaving him!

STEPHEN: He's but a shadow, anonymity
                  will keep him safe.

WENDY: With the dogs? He's my son.

STEPHEN: If he was it would be different. He's not.

                  (.)

WENDY: Why wouldn't, why won't you give me a child?

29

STEPHEN: It would have been irresponsible, let
              alone against the law.

WENDY: It's the one thing.

STEPHEN: You're the one that bangs on about setting
              an example. You understood. People
              abandoned their kids. They couldn't feed them,
              it was the responsibility of
              the State but the State could not afford
              luxuries like social care and food so
              the children ran wild, wild lost boys and girls.
              You said I should lead, lead by example
              and adopt. So we did. A few others
              followed suit but not enough, that's why they
              were collected, evacuated, why
              we didn't get pregnant, why we don't try.
              One rule for all, no exceptions for us.

WENDY: Except you're running away.

STEPHEN: It's over,
              unless of course you want to be found raped
              and decapitated in a storm pipe
              by the Thames?

WENDY: But Peter…

STEPHEN: Peter survived
              before he came to us, he'll forget soon
              enough. And yes, perhaps those dogs will be
              his friends.

WENDY: I love him, Stephen I love him.

STEPHEN: Of course you're fond of him, but I promise
              that when we're safe and settled I'll give you
              a baby of our own. You'll forget him.

WENDY: I won't, I won't, I can't.

STEPHEN: You'll have to. You will.

There is the sound of an explosion in the distance.

(.)

STEPHEN: They're killing each other. Killing themselves
to kill each other. Killing themselves to
kill each other to kill me. To kill this
country. They've won.

WENDY: No Stephen. Not like this,
clandestine in the middle of the night.

STEPHEN: It's so hot.

WENDY: You united them once. You
can do it again.

STEPHEN: How? How, Wendy how?

WENDY: Give them what they want.

STEPHEN: And what's that? Tell me.

WENDY: They want their children, they want food on their
table, they want clothes on their back, their husbands'
seed in their bellies. They want to work.

STEPHEN: Yes I agree they want all that and more,
tomorrow, but what do they want today?
Every time they take to the streets, every
time they loot and raid and rape and pillage
what are they looking for? What is it they
seek right now? Do you know?

WENDY: Do you?

STEPHEN: Blame. Blame.
More than food they hunger for blame; to point
the finger, to shift responsibility,
to say it's your fault not mine. That's how it
works, how society has always worked.
Until we fucked it all up.

WENDY: We haven't
done anything.

STEPHEN: Not me and you. Not just
me and you, all of us. We all said yes.
Yes you can do that, yes you can have that,
yes you can watch that, yes you can drink that,

yes you can try that, yes you can fuck that,
yes, yes, yes, fuck, fuck fuck and now we've fucked
ourselves into yesterday because yes,
today, it ends; today no one's to blame.

The electricity flickers for a moment, again the night lights blink.

STEPHEN: Except me.

WENDY: In that case we're all to blame.

STEPHEN: If it's not the Jews, it's the Catholics,
if it's not the Catholics, it's the Muslims,
if it's not religion it's the commies
or the Nazis or the students or the
bankers or the media or the gangs.

WENDY: Or the poor.

STEPHEN: And there's the rub. Because we're
all poor and we all have student debt and
we all wished secretly that we were the
bankers and longed for the protection of
a gang and we all read the newspapers
so that leaves a great big brush tarnishing
us all. But blame is specific. They want blood, the
blood of those who are to blame.

WENDY: A witch-hunt.

STEPHEN: Society in motion. You're right, I
united them once and it seems I've done it
again but at what cost? The death of a
pregnant woman, her unborn child removed
and missing. You know, for all the talk of
broken homes it's family that has been
the uniting force. A horrific
demonstration of the destruction
of the family unit. Perhaps it's not
just blame for which they hunger. Yearn. They crave
cohesion, solidarity, union.

WENDY: They want to be a nation.

Pause.

During the pause there is a lull in the chanting and fighting. They listen.

We hear a far off machine gun firing two short blasts. The external chaos resumes.

STEPHEN: I'll make arrangements for Peter to be
dropped away from the city.

STEPHEN begins to leave.

WENDY: That is it.
I think that's the explanation.

STEPHEN: For what?

WENDY: Those moments. Throughout all this, the last three
years, the times when we've despaired, when swathes
of the city burned, when it was every
man for himself. It explains those moments.

STEPHEN: Which moments?

WENDY: Those moments of unity.
At the beginning, when we allowed the
looting; smiles all round, lifting the secure
grills to help each other into the shops.
Then later when turf wars were forgotten,
rival gangs cooperating for days,
weeks, months against their common enemy, us.
And right now they know they're untouchable
because they're one. It explains those moments.
Those moments of beauty amidst the ugly.

STEPHEN: There is no beauty in loss of control.

WENDY: Control is never lost, only exchanged.
That's what I'm saying; in those shared moments
these people take back what little control
there can be in their lives, collectively
they remove the leash on which they feel bound.
Their shared destruction harnessed becomes a
positive force and the more often these

moments, the more often they're in control,
until we get to where we are now.

STEPHEN: Where's that?

WENDY: A precipice.

STEPHEN: No Wendy, we're not.

STEPHEN turns.

WENDY: This night will define history Stephen.
This night you could define history. Run
away and the country will literally
go to the dogs but harness these moments,
these moments of belonging and we will
rise from the flames a nation once more. You
already know for what they hunger, they
thirst for unity and blame. Unify
them in blame.

STEPHEN: But who's to blame if not me?

WENDY: The bastard who ripped an unborn child from
a dying woman's womb. Find that person,
find the child dead or alive and give the
people what they want.

STEPHEN: What's that?

WENDY: As you said. Blood.

The electricity fluctuates, the night lights and lamp flicker.

STEPHEN: Whoever it is has committed a
terrible crime but they aren't to blame for
society.

WENDY: The Jews, the Catholics,
and the Muslims were never to blame but
they were punished none the less. It's as you
said, blame is specific. This is your time
to specify.

STEPHEN: Vilify.

WENDY: To save us.

STEPHEN: Peter?

WENDY: The country. The nation. Us all.

STEPHEN: What you're talking about is folk devil.

WENDY: For moral panic. An eye for an eye.

STEPHEN: Have you lost your mind?

WENDY: We need a monster.

STEPHEN: I'm starting to think I'm looking at one.

WENDY: Fight fire with fire. Show them you mean business.

STEPHEN: Barbarism.

WENDY: Unite them in their hate
and their love for you will grow.

STEPHEN: Who are you?
You're actually suggesting we bring back…

WENDY: …hanging, flogging, firing squad if you / prefer.

STEPHEN: Wendy / I'm a liberal democrat!

WENDY: Liberal? Where has it got us? We can't coax
people out of this. Take a stand. Set an
example.

STEPHEN: You're talking about murder.

WENDY: I'm talking about doing whatever
is necessary in order for you
to retake control. The time for listening
has gone; we must condemn a little more
and understand a little less.

STEPHEN: I understand
It would make us the same as them.

WENDY: Would it?
Have you looted and robbed, arsoned and
pillaged, raped, murdered, stolen an unborn child?

STEPHEN: No.

WENDY: But someone has and they're desperate to blame.
You're right, this is how society works.

Society works when those in charge learn
when to say no. We've said yes for too long.
Yes we can? No you can't. What better way
to stop this madness than to say enough
is enough. Someone has that baby, dead
or alive, it does not matter, people
are rioting. Some sick bastard mutilated
its mother, they want that bastard's blood.
They're screaming but you won't listen and so
they'll come for you instead. Hear their voices,
respond with your own. 'If you kill, we'll kill you'.

*A large explosion is heard. Simultaneously the lights and
night lights flicker.*

Pause.

STEPHEN: You must really think you love Peter.

WENDY: What?

STEPHEN: To say these dreadful things.

WENDY: The world is full
           of dread Stephen.

STEPHEN: Capital punishment
           only ever creates more, we know that.

WENDY: The time for ideals is gone.

STEPHEN: It hasn't.

WENDY: Running away is your ideal is it?

STEPHEN: Protecting those I love.

WENDY: Yourself?

STEPHEN: You.

WENDY: Peter?

STEPHEN: He's not mine.

WENDY: You hate children.

STEPHEN: Far from it.

WENDY: You won't give me one.

STEPHEN: Wendy that's the law.

WENDY: You make the laws.

STEPHEN: Not for long. Come midnight
we'll be gone.

WENDY: Not without Peter.

STEPHEN: Baby,
we'll have our own.

WENDY: When?

STEPHEN: Soon as we're settled.

WENDY: You've said this before.

STEPHEN: I promise.

WENDY: Prove it.
Come on, if we're leaving tonight what does
it matter if your seed is in me or
not? All I have ever wanted, all my
life, is a baby Stephen, of my own.
If we're truly being driven away
by this crime, the theft of an illegal
babe, does one more unlawful foetus matter?
I'm your wife, in law. Legitimise me.
Legitimise us. Legitimise here.
                    (She places her hand on her stomach.)

(.)

*STEPHEN approaches, as he does he undoes his trousers and
hitches up WENDY's dress. He roughly enters her moaning
as he does. WENDY bites his shoulder to stifle her discomfort.*

STEPHEN: I can feel your sweat.

WENDY: Sorry.

STEPHEN: No, it's nice,
dirty.

WENDY: I'm a dirty girl.

STEPHEN exhales heavily as he starts to find his rhythm.

WENDY: Dirty girl
              has missed this…

              He grunts.

WENDY: …hardness stretching me inside.

              He kisses her roughly.

WENDY: Is dirty girl better than a wank, sir?

              STEPHEN changes position putting WENDY on the bed. The new position gives both of them pleasure.

WENDY: More sir…

              STEPHEN grunts as the rhythm increases.

WENDY: …this is what it's meant to be like,
              Mister Prime Minister. Dominant, in
              control, charging forth, harder…

              The pace increases further.

WENDY: …using me
              however you like.

              He kisses her roughly.

WENDY: You're running away.
              Scared to stake a claim over what is yours.

              STEPHEN enters her more deeply taking WENDY by surprise.

WENDY: Give me a child, a first daughter, first son,
              seed me Stephen with a child of your own.

              STEPHEN is almost lost in ecstasy as the rhythm increases further.

WENDY: Stay and show them, prove that you've got the balls.

              He moans – he's transfixed on reaching orgasm.

WENDY: That's it Daddy, give it your dirty girl.
              Punish me like you're going to punish
              that bastard. The big man coming to sort
              this out, coming to sort me out. Inside,

stay inside me always, inside this house,
inside your nation, inside my cunt-try,
show them like you're showing me now, prove it,
prove it to yourself, what a real man you are.

*STEPHEN suddenly changes position, as this happens we see
PETER's shadow in the doorway.*

WENDY: What are you doing?

STEPHEN: Daddy's dirty girl.

*STEPHEN spits on his hand and quickly enters her anally.
WENDY makes a sharp moaning sound. STEPHEN grabs her
by the hair and kisses her passionately, moaning into her
mouth as he orgasms.*

(.)

PETER's shadow withdraws.

STEPHEN withdraws from WENDY.

STEPHEN: I think I ripped your pants. Please take them off.

*WENDY removes her underwear. STEPHEN takes them and
wipes himself with them.*

STEPHEN: Clean.

STEPHEN passes the underwear back to WENDY.

STEPHEN: You'll need to wipe.

STEPHEN zips up and moves away.

WENDY: Why up my arse?
           A waste of good seed.

STEPHEN: Because you are right.
           What sort of man runs away? A coward.
           You said prove it to myself. We should stay.
           I'm the man they elected. I'm the man
           who can bring the people back together.
           I'm the man who will rebuild this nation,
           a nation built on family values.

This stolen infant needs to be found, its
thief robbed in return. Burgled of his life.

STEPHEN kisses WENDY.

STEPHEN: They say that don't they? Under every strong
man there lies an even stronger woman.

WENDY: A stronger woman whose womb is still ripe.

STEPHEN: One rule for all, no pregnancy until
our peace returns. Laws have failed, but they will
fail no more. I'll call this one Wendy's Law.
Wendy my love, you'll watch the bastard burn.

STEPHEN kisses her.

*For a moment there is a joyful sound amongst the outdoor
cacophony. The night lights blink. A helicopter passes close
by. STEPHEN exits.*

(.)

*WENDY wipes her bottom and the backs of her legs with the
torn underwear. She puts them in the laundry basket. The
Westminster chimes toll the passing of the half hour. She
approaches the air conditioning unit, briefly fiddles with its
controls but to no avail. She resumes tidying.*

*PETER enters silently, unnoticed by WENDY. He wears only
striped pyjama bottoms, his hairless torso exposed. It is
apparent by his body shape he will soon grow into a man.
PETER watches WENDY tidy.*

He dog barks, which scares WENDY.

WENDY: You scared me.

PETER dog barks.

WENDY: Stop that.

PETER dog barks.

WENDY: Peter please.

PETER dog growls.

WENDY: You're being silly.

PETER gets onto all fours and prowls.

WENDY: Peter stop that.

PETER dog barks.

WENDY: What are you doing?

PETER: Don't you understand? *(PETER dog barks.)*

WENDY: Stop barking.

PETER sniffs the air.

WENDY: What are you doing? I don't understand.

PETER: You should. *(PETER dog barks.)*

WENDY: Stop that, you're not a dog.

PETER: I know, Wendy. *(PETER dog barks.)*

WENDY: Stop behaving like one.

PETER howls.

WENDY: Stop it now Peter.

PETER: I'm not but you are. *(PETER dog barks.)*

WENDY: I don't know this game.

PETER: I'm not playing one. *(PETER dog barks.)*

WENDY: I'll call for Stephen.

PETER: Daddy? He's dog too. *(PETER dog barks.)*

WENDY: What's got into you?

PETER: What's got into you?
                                    (PETER dog barks.)

            I saw you and him, rutting, dogs do that.

*PETER barks. PETER wildly charges at WENDY on all fours,
at the last moment he stands bolt upright, face to face with
WENDY, almost touching. PETER is panting heavily.*

PETER: Was it good? *(He pants.)*

WENDY: It's what mummies and daddies do.

PETER: Is it? *(He pants.)*

PETER goes to touch WENDY between the legs but she grabs his hand, holding it back.

WENDY: No Peter.

(.)

PETER starts panting more heavily, at first onto WENDY's face then he begins to move around the room, each pant accompanied by a foot stomp.

WENDY: Peter…

PETER: Shut up I am concentrating.
                                         (He pants and stomps.)

WENDY: That won't work.

PETER pants more heavily, stamping harder.

WENDY: It doesn't work here.

PETER: I'm killing grown-ups.
                                              (PETER pants.)

WENDY: You'll hyperventilate.

PETER: *(PETER pants.)*
         If I kill enough I'm bound to get Steve.

WENDY: It doesn't work.

PETER pants.

WENDY: I'm not sure it's ever worked.

PETER stops and fixes his stare on WENDY.

WENDY: Anywhere. Ever.

Pause.

An ambulance siren passes on a road outside.

PETER: Told you. I'll stop now. I've killed quite enough.
         Hook handed man will get him anyway.

WENDY: I don't think so.

PETER: There will be blood tonight.

WENDY: You should learn to love your father Peter.

PETER: Why?

WENDY: So that he might learn to love you back.

PETER: Was that love?

WENDY: Was what love?

PETER: The dog love.

WENDY: Yes.

PETER: At my window Wendy?

WENDY: It's my window too.

PETER: I know.

WENDY: Do you?

PETER: There's always a window.

WENDY: This one's our window Peter. Me and you.

          (.)

WENDY: Peter?

PETER: Yes?

WENDY: Can you see that I'm different?
          Can you see that I'm a grown woman now?

PETER: Could you see every meal we ate?

WENDY: Peter…

PETER: Could you?

WENDY: No.

PETER: But you imagined. We can
          pretend.

WENDY: Not in this life, not in this time.

PETER: Then I'll go back.

WENDY: You think you could?

PETER: You'll see.

PETER concentrates. He closes his eyes and opens out his arms.
A smile spreads across his face.

PETER: I knew I could.

WENDY: Open your eyes Peter.

PETER does.

PETER: What's happening? Wendy what's happening?

WENDY: Nothing. Nothing's happening. You've forgot.

PETER runs around the room.

WENDY: You've forgotten Peter.

PETER climbs onto his bed and throws himself into the air.
He lands in a pile.

WENDY: It's been too long.

PETER: Shut up. I can remember everything.

PETER climbs up onto the window ledge.

WENDY: No.

PETER: I'll fly.

WENDY: Peter you won't.

PETER: Can. I will.

WENDY: You'll fall. You'll die.

PETER: So?

WENDY: Please Peter, get down.

PETER: I've only been here a week.

WENDY: A year.

PETER: Say you believe.

WENDY: No.

PETER: Say you believe or
I'll jump.

WENDY: If I say I believe you will.

PETER: Do you believe?

WENDY:	The question is, do you?

(.)

PETER gets down.

PETER:	It is easier by foot anyway.
WENDY:	Of course.
PETER:	I know where the park gardens are, I was there tonight, where Tinkerbell lives.
WENDY:	And was she there?
PETER:	It was full of pirates.
WENDY:	Was she there? Were there any other faeries there?
PETER:	No. I heard a man say there were often fairies in the bushes but I saw none. They've probably gone to the moon for the weekend.
WENDY:	It must be a long one?
PETER:	Suppose.

(.)

WENDY:	Peter, we must forget the before time.
PETER:	You're always telling me to remember.
WENDY:	Perhaps I am wrong.
PETER:	Are these feelings wrong? I can't forget what's inside me.
WENDY:	I know.

Pause.

WENDY:	How was your bath?
PETER:	Dangerous, I almost drowned, one of the mermaids from Marooner's Rock came through the plug hole.
WENDY:	I don't think so.

PETER: She took me deep under the water and whispered in my ear the strangest of dreams.

WENDY: You fell asleep in the bath?

PETER: I remember.

WENDY: You should be careful.

PETER: I'll tell you shall I?

WENDY: I'd love nothing more, but why don't you lie down whilst you do?

PETER: You can't trick me Wendy. I won't sleep until midnight past.

WENDY: It's late.

PETER: It's your birthday soon.

WENDY: You should be in bed.

PETER: Please, Mummy.

WENDY: Asleep straight after. Promise?

PETER: I promise.

WENDY: And you must sit on your bed.

PETER jumps onto his bed. WENDY goes to close the window.

PETER: Leave the window Mummy.

WENDY: But it's noisy.

PETER: Redskins are louder.

WENDY: The weather will break.

PETER: If it storms you can close the windows then.

WENDY: I suppose it does still feel very close.

WENDY sits on the bed with PETER.

(.)

WENDY: So tell me.

PETER: Tell you what?

WENDY: Your adventure.

PETER: Oh yes I almost forgot.

WENDY: The mermaid.

PETER: She whispered a funny dream into me.
          The Big Bird was eating her own eggs, they
          were full of blood and her eyes were wide like
          yours get when I see you in the middle
          of the night. When all the eggs were gone she
          laid back in her nest and floated on an
          ocean of tears but then she felt unwell.
          She had a knot in her stomach but it
          wouldn't sick up and the pain began to
          wrestle with her insides, her gullet was
          bulging and about to burst. She started
          to laugh and as she laughed a beak broke through
          her flesh from her innards, splattering gore
          across her feathers. The chick ragged its way
          through its mother's flesh, consuming her as
          it did and all the while the Wendy bird
          laughed ecstatic and in pleasure. When
          the bird was finally released from its
          fleshy warm fortress the bird was no longer
          bird but a boy, a boy that was changing,
          a boy that was angry and a boy that
          barked like a dog. Then my shadow woke me
          up and told me to come to you and play.
          What do you think it means?

WENDY: It's just a dream.

PETER: But dreams that vivid are rarely for nought.

WENDY: You're just processing the day's news.

PETER: What news?

WENDY: You haven't seen?

PETER: I don't like the world-casts,
          everything looks so unreal. What you do
          with your hands and your mind means so much more.

WENDY: I think Stephen and you will get on yet.

PETER: I doubt it.

WENDY: Just promise me you will try.

PETER: If he doesn't kill me first Wendy.

WENDY laughs.

WENDY: If I don't kill you first.

(.)

The electricity flickers and the night lights blink.

PETER: That was just another faerie dying.

WENDY: The power's weak.

PETER: When people give up, stop believing in their dreams, a light goes out.

WENDY: They'll believe again soon, Stephen has a plan Peter, you'll see.

PETER: I'm sure I will.

The lights blink.

(.)

PETER: Tell me a story.

WENDY: You're too old for that.

PETER: But it's bed time Wendy.

WENDY: No buts.

PETER: But.

WENDY: No.

PETER: I told you one, about my mermaid dream.

WENDY: No Peter.

PETER: It's not midnight yet. Please, please, Wendy. Mummy.

WENDY: Are you comfortable?

PETER: Like a bug in a rug.

WENDY: No interrupting.
There was once a gentleman…

PETER: Not a lady?

WENDY: This is Wendy's story Peter.

PETER: I would
have rathered it was a lady.

WENDY: There was
a lady too.

PETER: Does she die?

WENDY: Listen. There
was once a gentleman and a lady.
The gentleman could be very gentle
but he could also be very hard.
One day the man was particularly
cruel and told the lady he wouldn't give
her a child. This broke the lady's heart, all
she ever wanted was a descendant
of her own.

PETER: What's descendant? Is it like
the dogs?

WENDY: I suppose so yes, everything
descends.

PETER: Even you?

WENDY: The story Peter.

PETER: Is it like babies?

WENDY: Exactly.

PETER: So all
she ever wanted was a baby of
her own?

WENDY: Yes.

PETER: Brilliant.

WENDY: No it's awful.
Her husband said it was illegal.

PETER: Ooo.

WENDY: But then something marvellous happened.

PETER: A baby?

WENDY: The little boy came back.

PETER: She
descended?

WENDY: He came back.

PETER: Where had he been?

WENDY: Far away. In a land full of fun and
adventure.

PETER: And danger?

WENDY: And danger yes.

PETER: Were there pirates there?

WENDY: Yes.

PETER: And faeries?

WENDY: Yes.

PETER: And crocodiles?

WENDY: Yes.

PETER: And lots of children?

WENDY: Yes.

PETER: I knew it! I don't know how but I knew.

WENDY: Because you are a clever boy Peter.

PETER: Am I?

WENDY: Yes, soon you'll be a clever man.

PETER: What happened next?

WENDY: The lady was confused.

PETER: It is awfully puzzling.

WENDY: Because
she remembered the boy but from where she
did not know.

PETER: Had he been gone a long time?

WENDY: Many moons had past. She decided she remembered him from a forgotten dream.

PETER: She descended in a forgotten dream?

WENDY: A dream from when she was just a girl, on the eve of womanhood, a dream that brought her first blood, a dream of a boy who played mummies with her, a dream of love stolen kisses, butterflies here and when she woke her dream had returned.

PETER: Was her dream crying?

WENDY: He was.

PETER: I knew it. Did the lady cry?

WENDY: She had almost forgotten him you see.

PETER: What about the gentleman?

WENDY: She still loved him very much.

PETER: But?

WENDY: But something had stirred. Something the man would never understand.

PETER: I don't think I can see a happy end.

WENDY: If you knew how great this mother's love, you'd have no fear.

PETER: What did she do?

WENDY: The lady found a way to keep the boy as her own.

PETER: I knew that too! The gentleman grew hard?

WENDY: Though in time the little boy softened him.

PETER: Does the boy ever go back to his land?

WENDY: Let us take a peep into the future. There's the boy, but more grown, the shadow of manhood across his face, he walks with the

         lady and the gentleman, the picture-perfect
         family, an example for all.

PETER: What else do you see?

WENDY: What's that – could it be?

PETER: I knew there'd be something else.

WENDY: Yes it is,
         a perambulator, pushed along, what
         could be inside?

PETER: A baby?

WENDY: Yes indeed!

PETER: A gurgling baby of her own Wendy?

WENDY: A descendant.

PETER: Babies gurgle you know.

WENDY: They do.

PETER: At first. And cry. I know about
         babies you know.

WENDY: You do?

PETER: Of course. I know
         where they come from.

WENDY: I'm not quite finished yet.

PETER: Wendy, this is the part I hate the most.

WENDY: And they all lived happily ever after.

PETER: You didn't explain where she got the baby.

WENDY: She let the future take its course, Peter.

PETER: Did it grow from a seed? I know about
         these things. Seeds in bellies. A woman's blood.

WENDY: Father will have this talk with you.

PETER: Daddy?

WENDY: Yes.

PETER: Stevie boy?

WENDY: Stephen.

PETER: It's funny when
you get shy.

WENDY: Stop it Peter.

PETER: Our secret.

WENDY: There is no secret.

PETER: Mummies and daddies.
Wendy, the future's yet to take its course.

The night lights flicker.

(.)

WENDY makes to leave.

PETER: Where are you going?

WENDY: It's bed time Peter.

PETER: It's not your birthday yet.

WENDY: You're too tired.

PETER: I've got you a present.

WENDY: Give it to me
in the morning.

PETER: It has to be tonight.

WENDY: It's bed time.

PETER: It was in my dream Mummy, please.

*The Westminster Chimes toll the passing of the three quarter
hour.*

STEPHEN enters.

STEPHEN: Done, it's being ratified as we speak.

WENDY: No opposition?

STEPHEN: From the right or the
middles? I think not. There was no one left,
an empty chamber. We're on the brink of

> military rule, civil war. You're right.
> Come midnight Wendy, Wendy's Law will pass.

STEPHEN kisses WENDY.

PETER: What's Wendy's Law?

STEPHEN: We'll make the announcement tonight. The world-casts are deployed, schedules have been cleared.

WENDY: But have they found it yet?

PETER: What are you looking for?

WENDY: Found the bastard?

STEPHEN: The dogs had a scent.

WENDY: Had?

STEPHEN: They lost it in Kensington Gardens, too many people. They found some car keys though, covered in blood, the woman's blood.

PETER: What are you two talking about?

WENDY: He hasn't seen.

STEPHEN: There are some sick, sick people in this world Peter.

WENDY: Monsters.

PETER: Monsters are good!

WENDY: This is not a game.

STEPHEN: But he's right. This monster will save us. Save us all, you and me.

WENDY: And Peter?

STEPHEN: Him too.

The night lights blink.

STEPHEN: You were right. We need this. The country needs this.

WENDY: Not that word.

STEPHEN: The nation, our nation,
my nation needs this. An unflinching stance.
Wendy's Law will unite them all in blame.
Unify them in hate. Focus passion
and restore order to all.

WENDY: Unity
and passion? Sounds good Stephen, very good.

STEPHEN: I know.

(.)

PETER growls.

STEPHEN: Stop that! You should get changed, I want you by
my side.

WENDY: And Peter?

STEPHEN: An example?

WENDY: A
family.

PETER: Wendy it's just like your story,
all you need is the baby and a pram.

WENDY: The future will take its course.

STEPHEN: Peter put
some clothes on.

PETER: My Saturday's?

WENDY: Yes.

PETER: Will you
help me Mummy?

WENDY: No, but Daddy will.

PETER: But…

WENDY: Remember the story.

STEPHEN: Wendy…

WENDY whispers into STEPHEN's ear.

STEPHEN: Dirty.

WENDY: I hope I can trust you both to play nice.

WENDY exits.

Pause.

PETER: Are you a gentleman?

STEPHEN: I should hope so and one day you will be a grown man too.

PETER: What's Wendy's Law?

STEPHEN: A way to take control.

PETER: Wendy said you'd give me a talk.

STEPHEN: Really?

PETER: About descendants.

STEPHEN: What do you want to know?

PETER: I think I probably know already.

I know how to get them.

STEPHEN: Where they come from?

PETER: They come from ladies' tummies.

STEPHEN: Yes, that's right. Do you know how they get there?

PETER: They grow from a seed.

STEPHEN: That the daddy gives to them when he loves the mummy very much.

PETER: So the daddy gives the mummy a baby to show his love?

STEPHEN: Yes.

PETER: So you must not love Wendy?

STEPHEN: Of course I do.

PETER: But you haven't
given her a baby.

STEPHEN: No but I will.

PETER: You won't have to.

STEPHEN: What?

PETER: I'll give her one first.

STEPHEN's phone rings.

STEPHEN: What? What do you mean Peter?

PETER: You will see.

He answers.

STEPHEN: Yes? Hold on, the network's failing. Hello?
Yes, hello? I'm still here… Peter, get dressed.

STEPHEN exits.

(.)

*PETER begins to undo all of WENDY's tidying. He finds
WENDY's torn underwear, he sniffs at them like a dog. He
growls. He becomes more dog-like untidying the room on all
fours using his teeth. Perhaps he exposes the porn mag once
again. He catches the scent of his backpack and begins to sniff
at it. He starts to laugh.*

*WENDY enters in an elegant, fitted, black dress. She watches
him laugh.*

WENDY: Boy, why are you laughing?

PETER: I'm excited.

WENDY: What about?

PETER: Tonight.

WENDY: You have made a mess.

PETER: Are you mad?

WENDY: Only because you're not dressed.

PETER: Stevie's phone rang, beep beep, beep beep, beep beep.

WENDY: Fetch your Saturday's, if you can find them.

PETER: Is it Saturday?

PETER looks amongst his strewn clothing for his best, clean clothes. He starts getting dressed.

WENDY: Hurry.

PETER: Why dress up?

WENDY: You know why.

PETER: Because it is your birthday?

WENDY: We're going on the world-cast.

PETER: People will know who I am.

WENDY: They'll see you're our son. After tonight everyone will know who you are.

PETER: Yes, I think you're probably right.

The night lights blink.

WENDY helps PETER button his shirt.

PETER: I like this.

WENDY: Peter please.

PETER: You being mum. I think you'll make an excellent mother.

WENDY: I'm <u>your</u> mother.

PETER: Yes but not really, all you need is a baby of your own.

The night lights blink.

WENDY: We'll lose power soon.

PETER: Stevie will find a way.

(.)

WENDY finishes dressing PETER.

STEPHEN enters.

WENDY: Stephen? Stephen is everything alright?

STEPHEN: That was the Authority.

WENDY: You don't look well.

STEPHEN: They traced the car keys to a vehicle registration.

WENDY: Good.

STEPHEN: It was registered here.

WENDY: One of the staff?

STEPHEN: No, yours. They're your keys.

PETER giggles.

STEPHEN: Peter be quiet for a moment please.

WENDY: I don't think so.

STEPHEN: One of the staff must have taken them.

WENDY: Our car's not had fuel for months.

STEPHEN: They found your finger prints all over them.

PETER is giggling.

WENDY: My keys were in Kensington Park Gardens?

STEPHEN: Yes.

WENDY: Covered in the dead woman's blood?

STEPHEN: Yes.

WENDY: How did they get there? I've not left the house.

STEPHEN: That's what the Authority would like to know.

PETER laughs.

STEPHEN: Peter quiet, stop laughing, we're talking.

PETER laughs.

WENDY: We're not playing now it isn't a game.

PETER laughs.

STEPHEN: Shut the fuck up!

PETER suddenly stops laughing.

PETER: You two are so silly.

STEPHEN: Silly? A woman is dead, her unborn child removed and the only evidence the Authority has links the murder to your mother.

PETER: But Mummy didn't do it.

STEPHEN: I know that Peter.

PETER: Do you know who did?

STEPHEN: Of course not. The Authority is coming.

PETER giggles.

WENDY: Do you?

PETER smiles.

STEPHEN: I will wipe that smirk off your face.

PETER: It's not midnight yet.

STEPHEN: Do you know something?

PETER: It's not midnight yet.

WENDY: You said you hadn't watched the news.

PETER: World-casts are so unreal, it's always better to use your hands and mind.

WENDY: Do you know something Peter?

PETER: It's not time!

WENDY: That doesn't matter baby, if you know something it is better to tell us now.

PETER: I'm not going to bed.

WENDY: Stay up all night.

PETER: That's not going to happen.

STEPHEN: What do you know?

PETER: I have done you a favour Stevie.

STEPHEN: What?

PETER: You don't love Wendy.

STEPHEN: Of course I love her.

PETER: Not like I do.

WENDY: Peter please.

PETER: I've saved you
                the effort. The most bestest gift of all.

WENDY: What are you talking about?

STEPHEN: The car keys
                Peter, why were they in Kensington Park?

PETER: Because you had hidden the knives again.
                I needed something with a serrated
                edge. Keys are quite sharp you know. Be careful.

STEPHEN: What are you talking about?

WENDY: Peter?

PETER: You
                two are so silly. It was quite a lot
                of effort you know. The rock weighed a lot.
                I wanted her unconscious to stop her
                crying out. I bashed her until my arm
                ached. It's warm you know, blood, it splatters and
                sprays, it feels like you're in a red shower.
                A bit of her hair got stuck to the rock,
                that's when I knew to stop.

WENDY: This isn't the
                time for nightmares Peter.

PETER: *(PETER giggles.)* I know Mummy.
                She had to still be breathing otherwise
                there'd be no blood going to her tummy.
                She started to shake a bit, having a

fit, so I bashed her one last time. Her leg
twitched then she stopped. I thought I'd gone too far
but she took another breath so I started.

STEPHEN: Started what?

PETER: With the keys. I went too high
at first water came out. I think she had
just had a drink. But then I saw it kick,
it was like it was telling me where to
aim. I had to be quick it was getting
light. I knew she went walking before dawn
every morning, I've watched her. She was shamed
by her belly I think, an illegal.
She always cut across the car park and
she was always alone. I knew the rich
people's cars would come soon so I hurried.
There was a lot of blood, I think she pooed –
it smelt bad. I found it inside in a
translucent sack. I popped it. It gurgled,
then it cried. I pulled it out, I almost
dropped it because a dog came which made me
jump. He was letting me know there was a man.
I told him to go away, he licked the
blood off the woman's face then disappeared.
Did you know there's a tube attached to your
belly button? I didn't know what to
do with that because it was stopping me
taking it. I ripped it off using the
keys then went. I didn't have time to put
all the bits back inside the lady, that's
probably why she died.

WENDY: Where did you go?

STEPHEN: What did you do with the baby, Peter?

PETER: I went to the gardens. I needed to
keep it somewhere safe, secret, until
tonight, the faeries said they'd look after
it but they weren't there. I looked for them, that's
when I must have dropped the car keys. Sorry.

STEPHEN: Sorry?

PETER: I shouldn't have taken them but like I said I couldn't find any knives.

WENDY: Where's the baby now?

PETER: It's not midnight yet.

STEPHEN: Where is the fucking baby? Tell us now!

(.)

PETER goes towards his backpack.

PETER: Patience is a virtue you know Stevie.

PETER picks up his backpack.

PETER: You've ruined Wendy's birthday present now.

PETER gives the backpack to WENDY.

PETER: Here, happy birthday, hope you like it.

(.)

WENDY is frozen holding the backpack.

PETER: Are you not going to open it then? You're always saying how much you want one.

STEPHEN: Open it Wendy.

PETER: I suppose I should have wrapped it but you both insisted on having it before midnight.

STEPHEN: You have to open it Wendy.

WENDY slowly begins to unzip the backpack. PETER begins to giggle.

STEPHEN: Why are you laughing?

PETER: The look on both your faces.

STEPHEN: What?

PETER: Funny! You wouldn't think it was someone's birth-day.

PETER laughs.

STEPHEN: Stop laughing.

WENDY: Is this a joke? Not funny.

PETER: Open it you'll see.

STEPHEN: Fucking open it.

WENDY unzips the bag and looks inside. She is immediately repulsed, pushing the bag away from her. She wretches.

PETER: What?

PETER looks inside the bag, he puts the bag down disappointed.

PETER: I knew it would die. I didn't have anything to feed it. I'll probably have to walk with it to the stars, or at least until I see Tinkerbell. Sorry Mummy, don't be mad.

STEPHEN: What are you saying? Don't be mad?!

PETER: It's the thought that counts though, right? You could still put it in a pram and push it.

STEPHEN: Monster.

WENDY: Why Peter?

PETER: It's what you wanted.

WENDY: Not like this.

There is a massive explosion in the streets nearby followed by gunfire and sirens.

(.)

WENDY: Stephen. Wendy's Law.

STEPHEN: What about it?

WENDY: You've got to stop it.

STEPHEN: At midnight it is rule.

WENDY: Don't you see what it means?

PETER: It means he'll take
            control.

WENDY: He's just a child Stephen.

PETER: I thought
            I was a young man, Wendy?

WENDY: You're just a
            baby.

STEPHEN: He is thirteen.

WENDY: You know what will
            happen.

STEPHEN: There's nothing I can do.

WENDY: Stephen.

STEPHEN: He killed a mother and her child today.

PETER: What's Wendy's Law?

WENDY: Don't worry about that.
            Daddy's going to sort it out darling.

STEPHEN: Daddy is not going to sort it out.

WENDY: We'll be just as bad as...

STEPHEN: Who? As Peter?
            An eye for an eye. Take back control. One
            rule for one Wendy, one rule for all.

WENDY: You still have time.

STEPHEN: This is the example
            you're always talking about. Do as I
            say, do as I do, no one is above
            the law, not even you.

PETER: This is what the
            mermaid meant when she whispered in my ear.

STEPHEN: Mermaid?

WENDY: What else did she say?

PETER: That tonight
            I'd have the biggest adventure of them
            all, that I wouldn't see the dawn.

WENDY: Stephen
do something!

STEPHEN: I can't.

WENDY: You won't. You hate him.

STEPHEN: Quite the opposite. Thank you Peter, thanks.

PETER: Finally someone's grateful, it was hard
work getting that gift.

STEPHEN: Thank you. We are saved.

WENDY: Stephen, please.

STEPHEN: We're saved Wendy. We are saved.
Don't you see he's put an end to it all?
He'll unite them in hate, unify them
in grief, bond them in belief.

WENDY: What belief?

STEPHEN: In me. Peter will purge moral panic,
cleanse broken souls, this brutal act tonight
will restore peace and love to all.

WENDY: To all?
What about me, your wife?

STEPHEN: It's Wendy's Law.

A further explosion in the distance.

WENDY: Please.

*The Westminster chimes introduce the passing of the hour.
Big Ben tolls twelve times.*

(.)

PETER: Happy Birthday Wendy.

(.)

STEPHEN: Peter please come with me.

WENDY grabs at PETER.

PETER: Don't be frightened.

WENDY: You're going to die.

PETER: I've died lots of times.

WENDY: We're not playing.

PETER: Death's the best game of all.

STEPHEN begins to lead PETER away. PETER stops.

PETER: Wendy?

WENDY: Yes?

PETER: It's still there, in the corner
of your mouth, our secret thimble.

WENDY: I know.

(.)

WENDY blows the kiss. PETER catches it and holds it safe.

PETER: To die will be an awfully big adventure.
Come on Stephen, I think it's time to go.

PETER leaves the room.

(.)

STEPHEN tries to approach WENDY but she steps away.

STEPHEN exits.

Pause.

*We hear a distorted public announcement. The night lights
and room light begin to glow ever more brightly. We hear a
clap of thunder.*

Pause.

The cheering and chanting crescendos.

*WENDY goes to the window, removes her shoes and climbs up
onto the window ledge. The lights glow intensely. WENDY
looks down. The light bulb explodes.*

BLACKOUT.